objectifications ov estrangement

A.A.F.

Published by Arthur A. Filgueiras
Paperback ISBN 979-8-218-86477-4

Cover and sigil design by A.A.F.

objectifications ov estrangement third collection of poems by A.A.F.
It completes the cycle of descent begun in *the ephemeral nature ov* (Liber I-III)
and continued in *dissolutions ov refraction* (Liber IV-VI).

Illustration Credits:

All illustrations by Odilon Redon. Public Domain, sourced from the Internet Archive.

Image on page 12: "*Je vis une lueur large et pâle*" (1896).
Image on page 26: "*C'est le diable, portant sous ses deux ailes
les sept péchés capitaux*" (1888).
Image on page 38: "*La Muraille de sa chambre s'entr'ouvrait
et de la fente était projetée une tête de mort*" (1887)

these poems are a testament to my estrangement(s).

contents

VIII

I've often thought that there isn't any 'I' at all; that we are simply the means of expression of something else; that when we think we are ourselves, we are simply the victims of a delusion.

— Aleister Crowley,
Diary of a Drug Fiend

solve.

Liber VII:

the Quiet

?!

empty bed
still warm
(myself)

sits quiet.

breathing walls.
crackling air.

once alive.

libations
ov the mind.
minding

themselves.

surrounded
by flesh
in stillness.

no one is here.

space between
two selves
neither present

together alone.

our shadow
whispers

unseen voices.

body
without *mind*.

mind without
body.

happiness
sadness
unified

neither completing.

false eyes
reveal

learned eyes.

it(s) *not* here.
here is *not* it(s).

i'm not here.
where did you go?

we're not here.

where did you go?
you're not there.

where did (i) go?

Liber VIII:
the Shame

mirroring
a *shapeless*
shape

hates *it(self)*.

sickness
ov love
regurgitates

solitude.

warm night.
cold skin.
carved *out.*

straight i stand
bending to my

crooked self.

shamed ov flesh.

stench laces

was and is.

pain *full* ov body.
breathes
chokes

ov desolation.

melted
mask ov flesh.

beneath
mask(s) ov flesh.

defecating misery.

mask(s)
unable to hide.

split body.
halves vomit

together.

cordyceps
ov self

rots (*my*) control.

Liber IX:

dis-embodied

broken legs
walk *straight*.

down paths
forever bent.

passage
ov our flesh(s).

decaying
in time.

left to *splinter*
into a void.

contortion floats
alone.

chasing ghost(s)
only chases

itself(s).

hello *never*

arrived late
on time

to leave.

behind mirrors
silence

refracts *back*.

so far
(i) stay.

no further
we arrive.

still arrives
swallowing.

nothing remains.

unseen words

heard in
voiceless box(es).

silence.

filled by
pasts
never made.

time moves
unaware

(i) stand *dead.*

(?!)

solve

sine coagula.

objectifications ov estrangement

A.A.F.

all words were solely human written